Storms

Bernadette Brexel

Rosen REAL READERS

Rosen Classroom™
New York

Dark clouds are in the sky.
A storm is coming.

There are many kinds of storms.
Rainstorms bring rain.

Other storms bring snow.

A snowstorm brings snow.

A blizzard is a strong snowstorm.
It brings snow and strong winds.

Some storms have lightning
and thunder.
These are thunderstorms.

It is not safe to be outside
in a thunderstorm.

Sometimes it is very windy
with no rain or snow.
This is a windstorm.

Some storms pick up dirt and sand. These are sandstorms.

This storm is a hurricane.

It forms over the ocean.

Storms are very strong.
This tree fell over
in a strong storm.

Words to Know

clouds

hurricane

lightning

rain

snowstorm

windstorm